INSTITUTE FOR INTERNATIONAL ECONOMICS

PECIAL REPORT 6   DECEMBER 1987

RESOLVING THE GLOBAL ECONOMIC CRISIS:
AFTER WALL STREET

A Statement by Thirty-three Economists from Thirteen Countries

RESOLVING THE GLOBAL ECONOMIC CRISIS:
AFTER WALL STREET

Please accept this complimentary copy
for review. We would appreciate
receiving two copies of any notice or
review that you publish.
                    Thank you.

Pub. Date: 10/87   Price: $.300
Institute for International Economics
11 Dupont Circle, NW
Washington, DC 20036

SPECIAL REPORT 6

RESOLVING THE GLOBAL ECONOMIC CRISIS: AFTER WALL STREET

A Statement By Thirty-three Economists
From Thirteen Countries

INSTITUTE FOR INTERNATIONAL ECONOMICS
Washington, DC
December 1987

INSTITUTE FOR INTERNATIONAL ECONOMICS
C. Fred Bergsten, *Director*
Kathleen A. Lynch, *Director of Publications*
Ann L. Beasley, *Production Manager*

The Institute for International Economics was created, and is principally funded, by The German Marshall Fund of the United States.

The views expressed in this publication are those of the authors. The publication is part of the overall program of the Institute, as endorsed by its Board of Directors, but does not necessarily reflect the views of individual members of the Board or the Advisory Committee.

Printed in the United States of America   90 89 88 87   5 4 3 2 1

ISBN 0–88132–070–6

Contents

Preface

The world economy is obviously facing substantial difficulties. The huge imbalances in national current account positions—notably the American deficit and the counterpart surpluses in Japan, Germany, and the Asian NICs—have generated considerable instability in exchange rates and concerns over the sustainability of the economic expansion. The sharp decline in stock markets in late 1987, following the sharp decline in the American bond market earlier in the year, focused worldwide attention on these issues.

The Institute for International Economics therefore decided to bring together a number of distinguished economists from around the world to assess the situation, and to seek a common view on how best to respond. The group was chosen to reflect a wide range of philosophical viewpoints as well as all relevant geographical perspectives: North America, Europe, Japan, the Asian NICs, and Latin America.

The group met in Washington on November 23–24. It reached a surprising degree of agreement about the seriousness of the situation, the nature of the problem and the urgent need for policy changes in the United States and in many other countries. The group therefore decided to prepare a joint statement, covering the major aspects of the issue in some detail.

This statement—which contains many specific policy recommendations—speaks for itself. It concludes that "unless more decisive action is taken to correct existing imbalances at their roots, the next few years could be the most troubled since the 1930s." The statement is being released simultaneously in Brussels, Kiel, London, Paris, Rome, São Paulo, Seoul and Tokyo, as well as in the United States.

The Institute for International Economics is a private nonprofit research institution for the study and discussion of international economic policy. Its purpose is to analyze important issues in that area, and to develop and communicate practical new approaches for dealing with them. The Institute is completely nonpartisan.

The Institute was created by a generous commitment of funds from the German Marshall Fund of the United States in 1981, and continues to receive substantial support from that source. In addition, major institutional grants are now being received from the Ford Foundation, the William and Flora Hewlett Foundation, and the Alfred P. Sloan Foundation. A number of other foundations and private corporations are contributing to the increasing diversification of the Institute's financial resources.

The Board of Directors bears overall responsibility for the Institute and gives general guidance and approval to its research program—including identification of topics that are likely to become important to international economic policymakers over the medium run (generally, one to three years) and which thus should be addressed by the Institute. The Director, working closely with the staff and outside Advisory Committee, is responsible for the development of particular projects and makes the final decision to publish an individual study.

The Institute hopes that its studies and other activities will contribute to building a stronger foundation for international economic policy around the world. Comments as to how it can best do so are invited from readers of these publications.

C. FRED BERGSTEN
Director
December 1987

Resolving the Global Economic Crisis

1 THE ONSET OF THE CRISIS

The financial markets have given two very strong signals that something is seriously wrong in the world economy. First the bond market in the United States dropped by about 30 percent in the early months of 1987; then stock markets around the world plunged by 20 to 30 percent in late 1987.

The central problem is the existence of major and unsustainable imbalances. These take different forms in different parts of the world: the sizable budget and current account deficits of the United States, the large external surpluses of Japan and the Asian NICs, high unemployment in Europe, and indebtedness and stagnation in the developing countries.

The most glaring international imbalance—besides the undesirable transfer of real resources from indebted developing countries to richer industrial countries—is the growing indebtedness of the United States vis-à-vis the three main surplus areas: Japan, Europe—especially Germany—and the Asian newly industrializing countries (NICs), notably Taiwan.

The main danger today is that failure to correct these imbalances could lead to a serious world recession. The main opportunity today is that the corrective action needed in each country's own national interest would also help to correct the international imbalances.

The United States, primarily because of the sharp increase in the federal budget deficit since 1981, has been spending more than it produces, and investing more than can be financed by its inadequate savings. As a result, America's imports are now almost double its exports, and massive borrowing from abroad has converted it from the world's largest creditor country to the world's largest debtor.

1

On their side, the surplus countries have relied too much on export-led growth, and have also invested savings abroad that could often have been used more fruitfully at home. To varying degrees, most of them have significant underutilized labor and other resources, and substantial unmet social needs. In many European countries, especially, unemployment remains extremely high despite several years of recovery.

These internal and external imbalances have been widely—if not universally—recognized for some time. But the world economy maintained reasonably satisfactory growth with modest inflation, despite these imbalances, because private investors in the surplus areas were willing to finance American deficits at the going level of the dollar and US interest rates, rather than invest at home or in the developing countries.

In 1987, however, the situation changed dramatically. The net flow of foreign private savings into the United States dried up, particularly from Japan, triggering a sharp fall in the American bond market. Central banks stepped into the breach, increasing their foreign-exchange reserves by about $130 billion during the first 10 months of the year. This sharply increased money stocks in the surplus countries, inflationary fears reemerged, and interest rates rose around the world.

When disappointing American trade figures shattered the temporary lull induced by the appearance of currency stability under the Louvre Agreement, there were renewed fears of dollar depreciation, rising inflation and even higher interest rates. Equity prices plummeted around the world. The Federal Reserve—quite properly for the short term—pushed interest rates down in the wake of Wall Street's troubles, by creating substantial amounts of liquidity. But this is unsustainable for long if fundamental concerns about the dollar and the US budget deficit are not allayed.

The underlying imbalances can no longer be ignored. Indeed, continued failure to correct them courts the risk of a slide into recession throughout most of the world: in the United States via an excessive fall of the dollar triggering a renewed rise in interest rates, a new slide on Wall Street, and, in time, rising inflation; in the surplus countries through a precipitate further decline in their trade surpluses (due to the American downturn and sharp appreciation of their currencies) with multiplier effects on domestic investment and employment; and in the developing countries from a combination of the above. Such events could accelerate the already worrisome relapse into trade protectionism, and could return Third World debt to the crisis zone.

We thus believe that it is imperative to tackle the underlying problems forcefully, effectively, and urgently. The needed effort must begin in the United States, whose twin deficits lie at the heart of the matter. Policy changes in the surplus areas are also essential to restore stability, but are more likely to be forthcoming in the context of a much more vigorous American effort to deal with its own imbalances.

2 THE MAGNITUDE OF THE PROBLEM

The current account deficit of the United States is running at $150–160 billion a year. Views differ as to whether, to restore confidence in the dollar, it will be necessary to reduce it to zero so as to halt the buildup of foreign debt, or rather just reduce it sharply.

Some believe that it would suffice to initiate and achieve a steady reduction in the deficit to around 1 percent or so of GNP (about $50 billion at present), which would halt the rise in the ratio of foreign debt to GNP by 1990–91.

Others, such as the Joint Economic Committee of the US Congress, believe that the United States can restore full confidence only by reestablishing its traditional current account surplus, and that such a position is highly desirable in any event both for a country as wealthy as the United States (to permit it to export capital again) and for the leader of the free world (to avoid undermining its security role in both tangible and psychological ways).

Whichever view is taken, the required adjustment in the current account is substantial, ranging from $100 billion to $150 billion over the next four to five years.

On the other side, all the surplus areas will have to participate in this adjustment, because the inevitable correction of America's external deficit requires a widespread counterpart which no single area can provide. Based on the present distribution of current account surpluses, and their growth during the 1980s, the necessary reduction in these surpluses might be on the order of $50–75 billion for Japan, $30–50 billion for Germany, and $20–25 billion for the Asian NICs (see Table 1, p. 17).

An improvement in the Third World debt situation could help facilitate this adjustment. Any new financing arrangements that enabled the debtor countries to reduce their present outward transfer of resources would have their counterpart in improved trade balances in the rest of the world. Thus, the more it proves possible to channel additional funds to the debtor countries, the less the necessary reduction in the surpluses of the creditor countries.

It should be noted that the necessary shifts in *trade balances*, as opposed to current account balances, will be even larger. By 1990, the United States will be paying an additional $30–40 billion of debt service on an accumulated external debt of perhaps $700 billion, and the creditor countries will be earning a similar additional amount on their foreign assets. Thus, America's trade balance will have to improve by around $150–200 billion to bring the current account into the postulated range of minus $50 billion to zero, with corresponding swings elsewhere of $70–100 billion for Japan, $50–70 billion for Europe (largely Germany), and $30 billion for the Asian NICs.

These swings in trade balances will have a major impact on production and employment in the countries concerned. What is relevant in this context is the change in the *real*, or price-adjusted, trade balance, which is likely to be from 25 to 50 percent larger than the change in the nominal trade balance, depending on the country in question.[1]

For the United States, this means that the growth of domestic spending will have to be cut back sharply to leave room for an increased volume of exports and a lower volume of imports, equivalent to 4.5 to 6 percent of current GNP over four or five years. For Japan and Germany, it means that domestic spending, notably investment, will need to be boosted—by a roughly similar percentage of current GNP—to make up for a steep drop in the volume of net exports and to prevent a sharp rise in unemployment.

The challenge is to achieve these substantial adjustments in ways that will enable the world economy to keep growing at a rate of at least 2.5 to 3 percent a year. This is still short of the level that could be achieved if the large pool of unemployed and underemployed labor, especially in Europe and many developing countries, were effectively put to work.

But this growth rate should suffice to slow the rise in protectionism, and perhaps even allow its reversal. It should make it possible to avoid a renewed crisis over Third World debt. These policy areas require additional, specific initiatives. But a growth-oriented strategy is central to preventing them from erupting in ways that could jeopardize the adjustment process and severely damage the world economy as a whole.

It is also of cardinal importance that the international imbalances be corrected in a manner that preserves the hard-won victories over inflation of the first half of the 1980s. Indeed, this is one of the primary reasons to launch and complete the adjustment constructively—or else the United States, like many large debtors before it, could be tempted at some point to try to resolve its problem by inflating its debt away.

Excessive reliance should thus not be placed on dollar depreciation, especially in view of the key role the dollar plays in the world economy. Nor should the surplus countries be asked to expand beyond the capability afforded by their real resources, nor should they risk excessive growth of their money supplies through massive intervention in the currency markets.

3   PROGRESS TO DATE

The trade imbalances have levelled off in dollar terms. This considerable achievement is often ignored: the US current account deficit, for example, was

---

[1] This is because the fall in the dollar leads to a rise in US import prices relative to US export prices, so that in current (nominal) dollar terms a part of the benefit from the increased volume of exports and lower volume of imports is lost because of a deterioration in the terms of trade. Conversely, in the surplus countries, part of the loss from the lower volume of exports and higher volume of imports is offset by an *improvement* in the terms of trade.

headed toward an annual level of $300 billion or more by the early 1990s when the dollar was at its peak in early 1985.

Moreover, in volume terms, trade balances have begun to move in the right direction in almost all the major countries. The Japanese and German current account surpluses declined by more than 1 percent of GNP in real terms in 1986. The volume of US exports is up by over 15 percent during the past year, while nonoil import growth is flattening out. The US nonoil trade balance in real terms has improved by about 1 percent of GNP; it is improving faster than in 1978–80, and as fast as it deteriorated in the early 1980s.

To date, however, these volume gains have been largely masked by the price effects of the currency changes themselves. External imbalances in current dollars—which are what have to be financed—continue to grow (except for Japan during the past few months). The American deficit will be higher for 1987 than 1986 as will the surpluses of Germany, Taiwan, and Korea.

The shift in the volume of trade flows now under way will in time reduce the imbalances in current dollars, as price adjustments to the lower dollar are completed. But as of now, the likely improvement is not enough.

Before the further currency changes in the fall of 1987, the International Monetary Fund (IMF) and the Organization for Economic Cooperation and Development (OECD) were forecasting only a relatively modest reduction in the US deficit—despite a drop of over 30 percent in the trade-weighted dollar (measured by the IMF index). By early December, the trade-weighted dollar had fallen from mid-August by another 4 percent, but even allowing for this, it seems unlikely that on present policies the US current account deficit would fall much below $100 billion, and most projections show it rising again after 1989–90.

One critical point of timing must be recognized. Today's imbalances emerged over a period of at least five years, and will not be corrected overnight. Even on the most optimistic of scenarios, it will take four to five years to correct them. But the unmistakable message from the markets is that these imbalances have become unsustainable, posing a serious threat to the world economy. It is thus urgent to launch the adjustment effort now, although its implementation will take several years, and the full results will not come through until the early 1990s.

4   POLICY RECOMMENDATIONS

Our recommendations are divided into three parts: economic policy in each of the major countries, exchange rate relationships, and specific functional issues (trade and debt). National economic policies lie at the core of the problem, so we begin there.

National Economic Policies

For the *United States*, we have suggested that the objective should be to improve the trade balance by the equivalent of 4.5 to 6 percent of GNP in *volume* terms. This requires holding the growth of domestic demand below the growth of output by 1 to 1.5 percentage points for four or five years—a reversal from the past four years, when domestic demand exceeded output by an average of 1.2 percent annually. Capacity utilization is quite high, and unemployment is back to its level of the 1970s, close to what many of us believe to be the "natural rate." So, with shaky financing of the external deficit via unsustainable capital inflows, the United States now confronts a classic balance of payments adjustment problem.

In principle, the needed cutback in domestic demand could be achieved by restraining private consumption, private investment, or net government spending. However, substantial new investment will be needed in export and import-competing industries to support the necessary improvement in the trade balance. Consumer demand, after the sharp drop on Wall Street, may weaken somewhat, and the household savings rate may move back toward its traditional level, which would help finance the needed increase in net exports and investment.

But policy will have to achieve the bulk of the required redistribution of resources. The aim should be to achieve a balanced "structural" budget by FY 1992.[2] Prior to the November agreement between the administration and Congress, the FY 1988 deficit would have been roughly $180 billion, or 4 percent of GNP. This is virtually equivalent to the structural budget deficit since unemployment is currently close to America's natural rate.

The debate on the FY 1989 budget will resume early in 1988 and should be concluded as rapidly as possible. The goal should be a cut of at least $40 billion in the structural budget deficit below the FY 1988 level which, if the November agreement is fully implemented, should be around $160 billion, with further cuts of around $40 billion in each of the following three years. This timetable is only slightly more ambitious than the one called for under Gramm-Rudman, but as currently structured, that law has many weaknesses and cannot be relied upon to achieve its stated objectives.

To restore confidence in the currency, bond, and equity markets, it is essential that Congress legislate *in advance* the expenditure reductions and tax increases whose progressive introduction would eliminate the structural budget

---

[2] We wish to emphasize that the cuts should be calculated and implemented in terms of the structural, not the actual, budget deficit. If the actual budget deficit does not fall as much as expected because of a weaker level of economic activity, as is quite possible, this can and should be ignored as long as a credible program to reduce the structural deficit to zero by the early 1990s is firmly in place and being implemented faithfully.

deficit by the early 1990s—i.e., over the period during which the international imbalances need to be corrected. On the expenditure side, this could perhaps best be done by altering the formulas used to determine benefits under entitlement programs, or their tax status, or both.

Against this yardstick, we consider that the November 1987 agreement between Congress and the administration was grossly inadequate. The agreed "cuts" would leave the structural deficit in FY 1989 no lower than its present level, and some $30 billion short of the target suggested above. They include several "soft" features, such as one-time asset sales and assumed speedups in tax collection. They remain to be implemented.

Despite the obvious political difficulties involved, we urge the Administration and the Congress to go back to the drawing board. We note that significant budget packages, including tax increases, have occurred in two of the last three election years so that action cannot be ruled out on that account.

Politically, the most feasible budget package will probably include some mix of defense spending cuts, nondefense spending cuts (including entitlement programs), and tax hikes. The specific components of the budget package are less crucial than its total magnitude and launching it quickly and credibly. But it is important that any expenditure or (especially) tax changes should promote savings and investment, in preference to consumption, because of the importance of boosting the national savings rate and expanding investment— particularly in the tradables sector. The most critical requirement is to restore confidence in the fiscal probity of the United States, not least so that fiscal policy will again become available in helping extricate the country from a future recession.

Taken by themselves, such significant cuts in the budget deficit would tend to depress the US economy. But, as we have noted, the lower dollar is already giving it a strong boost that will continue for several years.

Equally important, we believe that the US budget deficit has been a significant factor, among others, behind the abnormally high level of long-term real interest rates in recent years, not only in the United States but also elsewhere in the world. Thus, once the financial markets become convinced that the US budget problem is being resolved, it should become possible to stabilize the dollar at an appropriate level with a somewhat lower level of US interest rates, while at the same time the Federal Reserve could return to a more steady—growth-supporting but noninflationary—rate of money creation.

Indeed, we consider that one of the prime objectives of the policies we advocate is to make it possible to bring down real long-term interest rates around the world, without requiring the world's central banks to indulge in excessive money creation—which would quickly be self-defeating. True, such a decline could prove short-lived if the policies we propose were to unleash the worldwide investment boom we would like to see. But this would be a cause for rejoicing rather than concern.

All in all, therefore, we believe that the depressive impact of the budget cuts proposed for the United States would be offset quite soon by the boost from a lower dollar and lower interest rates, and hence pave the way—probably after a temporary slowdown—to a subsequent period of faster growth.

Indeed, we would stress that *now* is the right time for significant cuts in the budget deficit. The real economy is still in good shape. If the deficit is not cut back to make room for increased net exports, inflationary demand pressures could quickly emerge; while if nothing is done about the budget deficit, then, over time, evaporating confidence in the financial markets could depress domestic demand in the least desirable way, via a recession.

Japan faces the opposite challenge: converting an economy traditionally driven by exports to a focus on domestic demand and boosting the productivity of domestically oriented output in the way that export-oriented output has thrived in the past.

It may remain appropriate for Japan to run a modest current account surplus, on the order of 1 to 1.5 percent of GNP (about $25–35 billion at present), in light of its high (if declining) savings rate and somewhat lower potential for domestic investment. And Japan will probably always run a bilateral surplus with the United States, given its dependence on imports of primary products and need to export to other high-income countries. But the overall current account surplus will need to be reduced by $10–15 billion a year over the next four to five years. This will require a larger reduction of its trade surplus—perhaps eliminating it altogether—in light of the rapid rise of Japan's overseas investment income as the world's largest creditor country.

The magnitude of the adjustment needed is substantial. To offset the decline in the trade surplus, domestic demand will have to rise by 1 to 1.5 percentage points a year faster than GNP—or at an annual rate of 4.5 to 5.5 percent—if unemployment is not to rise.

Japan has extensive unmet needs that can fuel a sustained reorientation toward domestic demand. The housing stock, in particular, requires extensive further modernization. Opportunities for additional infrastructure investment abound. Deregulation in such key sectors as agriculture, urban land use and trade policy offer substantial possibilities. The two Maekawa reports have described how Japan can achieve the needed reorientation, both providing a standard of living for its people in line with their remarkable productivity and harmonizing its economy far better with the rest of the world.

Three sets of measures can foster this transformation. National macroeconomic policy, including exchange rate policy, should continue to support the growth of domestic demand and provide price incentives to firms to orient their activities in that direction. Second, microeconomic policies—particularly regarding land use, taxation, agricultural policy and regulation (including import restraints)—need to reinforce the thrust of macroeconomic policy. Third, the firms themselves should redirect their activities toward the national market—

as many are already doing to a significant extent—and can speed the overall adjustment in some cases through direct investment abroad.

Fortunately, the adjustment process is off to a very good start. Domestic demand, spurred by the 6 trillion yen stimulus program in May 1987, is currently rising by 4.5 to 5 percent. A further boost may be needed, however, to sustain the adjustment over the next few years and offset the recent further appreciation of the yen. This could be achieved by a combination of deregulation, additional tax cuts, and public—or joint public-private sector—investment projects.

Such fiscal action should be designed to stimulate domestic demand in ways that are consistent with maintaining the structural budget deficit at a sustainable level over the medium run. This should be feasible because the present structural deficit (general government) is below this level, and because proceeds from the sale of NTT (Nippon Telephone and Telegraph) can be used to finance a temporary increase above it.

Europe presents a quite different picture, with high unemployment and slow growth. Globally, Europe is exporting capital that could be usefully deployed at home—1 percent of GNP for the European Community, but 3 percent for Germany. Growth forecasts for Europe have been revised down to less than 2 percent for 1987 and 1988 (and for Germany to 1.5 percent, according to the German Council of Economic Advisers). There is thus considerable supply-side potential for replacing export demand with domestic expenditure, notably investment, with total domestic expenditure growing 1 to 2 percentage points faster than now expected for at least the next two or three years.

In the international context, it is important to recognize that faster growth in Europe hinges especially on faster growth of domestic expenditure in Germany. From 1983 to the first half of 1987, DM 55 billion—or 80 percent— of the rise in Germany's overall trade surplus was vis-à-vis other West European countries. In part, this is why, despite the emergence of a massive US current account deficit, the current account positions of most other European countries, including France, Italy, and the United Kingdom, are now close to balance or in deficit. They therefore fear that, if they expand alone, the main result will be a rapid deterioration in their trade position and hence a need for early retrenchment.

For this reason, the only realistic and sustainable path to faster growth in Europe as a whole is through simultaneous expansion in all those countries which, individually, have scope for faster growth. Such simultaneous expansion is also needed to facilitate and offset the necessary correction of the US trade deficit. It should be accompanied by "supply-friendly" measures to minimize the risk that bottlenecks choke off growth or reignite inflation.

In the early 1980s, the monetary rectitude of the Bundesbank made an important contribution, via the European Monetary System (EMS), to bringing down inflation throughout Europe. Since 1985, however, the operation of the EMS has dampened the rise in the DM and made possible a massive rise in Germany's trade surplus with its European trade partners. Thus a period of "catch-up" growth in Europe as a whole may require not only a significant boost to German domestic demand, but also an upward realignment of the DM in the EMS, and a willingness on Germany's part to go into current account deficit for a while.

Faster growth in Europe would impart considerable impetus to the world economy as a whole. The Community is a large importer, particularly of primary products, and faster growth there stimulates both export volumes and prices throughout the developing world. This, in turn, translates into higher demand for American exports, thereby contributing considerably to the global adjustment, even though Germany alone, for example, conducts relatively little trade directly with the United States. The Community, as a group, could temporarily swing into external deficit for a period, reimporting some of the domestic savings that have flowed abroad so as to be able to finance the investment needed at home to reduce unemployment.

The German government recently announced an expanded program of subsidized credit to local authorities and small and medium-sized industries. While this measure goes in the right direction, more vigorous fiscal action is needed. The tax cuts now planned for 1990 should be brought forward and expanded in scope. These measures have already been thoroughly prepared as part of a medium-term program. But their timing was determined without reference to subsequent currency and other international developments, which have slowed German growth and now call for more rapid offset via domestic demand.

In addition to the planned tax cuts, and in view of the need to boost investment and bring down unemployment, Germany should also consider a temporary increase in depreciation allowances, a reduction in social security taxes on employment, or both. Further tax reductions could be envisaged if the government were prepared to embark on a program of progressively cutting subsidies to agriculture and industry.

Monetary policy in Europe is now quite expansionary, as evident in the growth of money supply and the recent round of coordinated cuts in short-term interest rates. As indicated above, we believe that once decisive action is taken to cut the US budget deficit, a worldwide lowering of real long-term interest rates should become possible without inflationary money creation. This would be especially welcome in Europe—and should be encouraged—because of the need to stimulate investment.

In the countries of Southern Europe, where budget deficits remain excessive and recent anti-inflationary gains need to be consolidated, there is little scope for autonomous expansionary action. In many other European countries, however, faster growth in Germany would open up scope for such action.

On the tax side, priority should be given to boosting employment, in particular by reducing the tax wedge between labor costs and take-home pay. On the expenditure side, there is a need to step up infrastructure investment—including some European projects in transport and communication—which has been held back by fiscal austerity in recent years. Wherever possible, this should be financed through the private sector (as for the Channel Tunnel) or through the European Investment Bank and the European Development Fund, so as to avoid an additional burden on national budgets.

Last, but certainly not least, real progress in creating a "single European market" for both trade and finance would greatly facilitate and spur the necessary shift in resources from declining net exports to America into employment-creating investment, designed to take advantage of the opportunities opened up by a more integrated European market.

Such a coherent program for expansion and lower unemployment would clearly be very much in Europe's own interests. It would also make a major contribution to maintaining growth in the world economy during the difficult period ahead when the United States is correcting its twin deficits. With the appreciation of its exchange rates, and strong competition from outside, the next few years provide a unique opportunity for Europe to achieve these goals without reigniting inflation.

The *Asian NICs* differ considerably among themselves, and all differ sharply from Japan (mainly because of their much lower levels of per capita income and much less advanced industrialization). Only Taiwan has run a consistent current account surplus since 1981, and its surplus and level of foreign-exchange reserves—the third largest and largest in the world, respectively—are far higher than those of the other NICs. Korea has a lower per capita income than the other NICs and remains one of the largest debtor countries in the world, although the current account surplus that emerged in 1986 became considerable in 1987, and Korea is now reducing its debt burden rapidly. Both Taiwan and Korea retain an extensive array of import barriers, though both have begun to reduce them aggressively, whereas Hong Kong and Singapore maintain virtually no trade controls.

We believe that the NICs, notably Taiwan and to a lesser degree Korea, should aim to greatly reduce their current account surpluses over the next three to five years. These countries have achieved the most enviable development records in the world over the past twenty years, and there is no reason why they cannot continue expanding their exports rapidly. However, in light of their relatively low levels of per capita income, the impressive rates of return on domestic investment and the threats posed to their monetary stability by continued large surpluses, it would be economically and politically unwise for them to continue running such large surpluses—which now exceed 20 percent of GNP for Taiwan and 8 percent of GNP for Korea. Thus, they need sharp increases in imports and some diversion of productive output to the domestic market.

Three sets of measures would seem appropriate for these countries. First, for Taiwan and Korea, there remains considerable scope to extend the program of trade liberalization. High tariffs and extensive nontariff barriers have become anachronistic for such dynamic exporters, both in economic terms and in light of the pressure in many industrial countries to erect new restraints on imports from them. The experience of Hong Kong reveals the value, in terms of avoiding protectionist reactions abroad, of maintaining a liberal trade regime at home.

Second, all these countries have enormous opportunities for further increases in domestic investment and thus in internal demand. Taiwan, for example, needs extensive new antipollution programs, highway systems, education and health facilities, and social insurance networks—so should no longer export half its savings. There is ample scope to maintain rapid growth while reorienting the economies away from trade surpluses. We would certainly not criticize the high rates of savings in these countries (or in Japan), but would seek to promote their deployment domestically in pursuit both of the countries' own interests and of better international balance.

Third, some further currency appreciation will undoubtedly be needed in the NICs to complete these adjustments. Their failure to appreciate much so far has slowed the international adjustment effort, as they have picked up market shares from Japan (and, to a lesser degree, Europe) due to the weakening of their currencies vis-à-vis those regions.

Such appreciation should be regarded as one of the payoffs—in terms of higher standards of living and lower inflation—for their hard work and successful development. The examples of Japan and Germany show clearly that stronger currencies need not undermine a country's international competitive position over the longer run, as they would surely not in these countries.

Exchange Rates

Substantial uncertainties surround the effects of the adjustment measures taken to date, the impact of the further steps suggested here, and the nature of the policy changes that will actually be adopted. Hence, it would be a mistake to attempt to stabilize exchange rates at the present time. If all the measures recommended above are adopted promptly and implemented faithfully, however, we believe that it should be possible to achieve the required adjustment with only modest further changes in exchange rates.[3]

Some further appreciation of the currencies of the Asian NICs, of the DM within the framework of the EMS, and of the yen, may be needed. But our

---

[3] At the time this statement was completed the dollar stood at 133 yen and DM 1.66, and the IMF trade-weighted index for the dollar at 101.5 (1980 = 100).

best guess is that in real trade-weighted terms the dollar may now be within 10 percent of a level consistent with the adjustment aims set out above.

At the same time, it would be highly undesirable for the dollar to fall excessively—overshooting on the downside as it did so substantially on the upside in the first half of the decade. On two key criteria, therefore, we believe that the monetary authorities of the countries concerned should stand ready to resist a further significant depreciation of the dollar. The criteria are (a) the adoption of a convincing policy package along the lines proposed here, by both the United States and the surplus areas, and (b) a commitment by the Federal Reserve to follow a noninflationary monetary policy, maintaining an appropriate interest-rate differential in favor of the dollar for as long as necessary to restore confidence in the currency markets.

We would emphasize that we are not suggesting that the dollar should be pegged at any specific level in nominal terms for any length of time, since it may well prove necessary to revise agreed support levels as the adjustment process proceeds. Moreover, if the measures proposed above were not adopted to any significant extent, then the dollar could fall a lot further, and attempts to prevent it from doing so would be fruitless.

In our view, such a sharp further fall in the dollar would *not* contribute constructively to the adjustment process. As so many countries have learned to their cost, currency depreciation that is not accompanied by strong action to slow down domestic demand simply paves the way to further currency depreciation. A further sharp fall in the dollar—by increasing inflation in America and the threat of recession elsewhere, and further undermining confidence in the world's key currency—could lead to a financial crisis and a serious world recession. Indeed, it is particularly because of these dangers that we believe the national measures described above are so greatly in the interests of both the countries concerned and the world economy as a whole.

Whatever level of exchange rates turns out to be needed to correct the present imbalances, the experience of sharp currency swings in the 1980s— which produced such large misalignments, and now requires such sizable adjustment in the opposite direction—clearly suggests the need to seek to improve the international monetary system. Just as we would not wish to see the dollar overshoot to an excessively depreciated level, we would not want to see it rise again prematurely—before the essential current account adjustments had been given time to eventuate and take hold.

Thus, as the adjustment process proceeds, businessmen in America and in the surplus countries need to be assured that the cycle of excessive currency fluctuations since 1973 has been tamed, and that a sensible pattern of real exchange rates can and will be maintained over the medium run. This is essential to provide them with a firmer basis for the longer term investment decisions needed to consolidate the adjustment process, and to promote growing world trade based on genuine comparative advantage.

Any improvement in the international monetary system should thus seek to place limits on the scope of future currency movements, to avoid substantial misalignments and to minimize unnecessary volatility. It should seek to preserve maximum freedom for both trade and capital transactions. And it should bring sufficient influence to bear on national economic policies to promote enough compatibility among them to deter the creation of large misalignments.

There are several potential routes to monetary reform. Some of us favor the introduction of a system of target zones, once a sustainable pattern of exchange rates has been established and reasonably validated by the markets. Whatever the route chosen, the crucial point is that while the system should be designed to promote internationally consistent national policies, it should not try to peg exchange rates at levels inconsistent with the national policies actually adopted. As we have stressed, greater stability of real exchange rates is needed to give businessmen around the world a better foundation on which to base their investment strategies at home and abroad. But attempts to stabilize exchange rates cannot provide this assurance unless they are backed by a genuine political commitment to follow macroeconomic policies consistent with such greater stability.

The world has experienced a series of crises of growing proportion under both the fixed-rate regime of Bretton Woods and the floating regime since 1973. It must be possible to do better. There is a strong tendency to forget the system once the crisis of the moment has been overcome, and we urge a more farsighted approach on this occasion.

Trade and Debt

The present crisis also requires further efforts to find constructive solutions to the steady rise of protectionism and the continuing threats posed by Third World debt.

On *trade*, it is imperative that the United States reject any legislation that could be viewed as protectionist. Indeed, such a step would be the height of folly for the United States just as its competitive position is improving and it seeks a $150–200 billion gain in its trade balance, because it would surely trigger retaliation from countries that are both prospering less than America and which now must accept large declines in their trade positions.

Beyond the trade policy problems involved, passage of such legislation could again contribute to instability in the financial markets—as when the dollar fell sharply in early 1987 on the occasion of both the semiconductor retaliation against Japan and House passage of the Gephardt amendment. Protectionist moves, especially by the largest country in the system and the traditional defender of open trade, would raise the ominous specter of the 1930s.

More positively, all major countries need to adhere scrupulously to the Standstill Agreement against new trade barriers reached in September 1986. Equally, they should push ahead as quickly as possible with the Uruguay Round to renew the postwar trend toward trade liberalization; strengthen the ability of the General Agreement on Tariffs and Trade (GATT) to handle the growing volume of trade disputes among its members; and write new rules to cover trade disputes in areas not now effectively governed by the GATT at all (notably agriculture, services, and investment).

A more vigorous effort to reform the common agricultural policy of the European Community would also be highly desirable, yielding important benefits to Europe's own welfare and to the world's more efficient agricultural exporters.

On *debt*, substantial increases in the flow of external resources to the developing countries are essential to enable them to restore acceptable rates of economic growth while continuing to service their debts. The industrial countries will thus need to find ways to restore significantly higher flows of capital to those debtor countries capable of putting them to productive use. This is not only in the best interests of the creditors and debtors, but, as noted earlier, would enable the developing world to make at least a modest contribution to the global adjustment process.

It is particularly important that Japan, with its large current account surplus, substantially increase both the level and concessionality of its transfers to the developing countries—to speed their growth and, especially via Latin America, to contribute indirectly to reducing the US trade deficit. Since most of the Japanese surplus accrues to the private sector rather than to the government, official action to spur such recycling may have to encompass tax incentives and partial guarantees to redirect the funds in the desired direction.

These trade and debt proposals interact with each other, as well as with the national economic policies suggested above. A restoration of forward movement on trade will provide the debtor countries (and the Asian NICs) with greater confidence that their export-oriented strategies will continue to work in practice. Steady progress on debt will reduce the risk that trade credits will dry up and further constrain world commerce—with detrimental effects on the global adjustment process—as well as the broader risks to the world's financial system. Maintenance of steady world growth would, together with the lower dollar, greatly benefit the debtor countries, particularly if accompanied by a decline in real interest rates. All these steps are part of the package needed to restore confidence to the world's financial markets and create a stable outlook for the world economy.

5   CONCLUSION

As noted at the outset, the financial markets have conveyed two very strong signals of the need to redress the fundamental imbalances now present in the world economy. We would underline the need for measures of adequate magnitude. Half-hearted steps will not do the job. Indeed, the magnitudes required to calm the markets grow disproportionately as their adoption is delayed. The costs will rise rapidly as long as effective action is postponed.

We would also stress the complementary nature of our proposals, which are mutually reinforcing at both the geographic and functional levels. Geographically, the twin deficits of the United States are the largest problem, but it is also in the interests of the surplus countries—both industrial and industrializing—to do their part as well if the adjustment is to succeed. Functionally, it is essential to move on several fronts: national fiscal and monetary policies, exchange rates, trade and debt. The nature of the problem cuts across all these countries and problem areas, and can be resolved only with a similarly comprehensive set of measures.

Since October 19, steps in the right direction have been taken in both America and the surplus areas. But they do not go nearly far enough. Nor can international meetings make up for inadequate national policies. Unless more decisive action is taken to correct existing imbalances at their roots, the next few years could be the most troubled since the 1930s.

TABLE 1 **ILLUSTRATIVE ADJUSTMENT OF NATIONAL CURRENT ACCOUNT POSITIONS, 1980–81 to 1991–92**
(annual average, billion dollars)

	Actual 1980–81	Estimated 1986–87	Targeted 1991–92
United States	5	−150	0 to −50
Japan	0	85	10 to 30
Germany	−10	40	−10 to 10
Taiwan	0	18	0 to 10
Korea	−5	7	0 to 5

SIGNATORIES

MICHEL ALBERT
President, Centre d'Etudes Prospectives et d'Informations
 Internationales (CEPII)
France

VICTOR ARGY
Professor of Economics, Macquarie University
Australia

C. FRED BERGSTEN
Director, Institute for International Economics
Former Assistant Secretary for International Affairs, Treasury Department
United States

BARRY BOSWORTH
Senior Fellow, Brookings Institution
Former Director, Council on Wage and Price Stability, Executive Office of the
 President
United States

WILLIAM R. CLINE
Senior Fellow, Institute for International Economics
United States

RICHARD N. COOPER
Professor of Economics, Harvard University
Former Under Secretary for Economic Affairs, Department of State
United States

DAVID A. CURRIE
Professor of Economics, Queen Mary College, University of London and
 Centre for Economic Policy Research
United Kingdom

THIERRY de MONTBRIAL
Director, Institut Français des Relations Internationales (IFRI)
Former Head of Policy Planning Staff, Ministry of Foreign Affairs
France

RIMMER de VRIES
Senior Vice President, Morgan Guaranty Trust
United States

RUDIGER DORNBUSCH
Professor of Economics, Massachusetts Institute of Technology
United States

JACQUES DREZE
Professor of Economics, Université Catholique de Louvain
Chairman, Macroeconomic Policy Group, Centre for
  European Policy Studies
Belgium

HERBERT H. GIERSCH
Professor, Institut für Weltwirtschaft, Kiel University
Federal Republic of Germany

DAVID D. HALE
First Vice President and Chief Economist, Kemper Financial Services
United States

JOHN F. HELLIWELL
Professor of Economics, University of British Columbia
Canada

PETER B. KENEN
Walker Professor of Economics and International Finance, Princeton University
United States

LAWRENCE R. KLEIN
Benjamin Franklin Professor of Economics and Finance,
  University of Pennsylvania
Nobel Prize for Economic Science, 1980
United States

BON-HO KOO
President, Korea Development Institute
Korea

EDMOND C. MALINVAUD
Professeur au Collège de France
Former Director, National Institute of Statistics (INSEE)
France

PAUL W. McCRACKEN
Professor Emeritus, University of Michigan
Former Chairman, Council of Economic Advisers
United States

STEPHEN MARRIS
Senior Fellow, Institute for International Economics
Former Economic Adviser to the Secretary-General, Organization for Economic
  Cooperation and Development
United Kingdom

MARCUS H. MILLER
Professor of Economics, University of Warwick and Centre for
    Economic Policy Research
United Kingdom

ISAMU MIYAZAKI
Chairman, Daiwa Securities Research Institute
Former Vice Minister, Economic Planning Agency
Japan

FRANCO MODIGLIANI
Institute Professor, Massachusetts Institute of Technology
Nobel Prize for Economic Science, 1985
United States

RICHARD O'BRIEN
Chief Economist, American Express Bank
United Kingdom

SABURO OKITA
Chairman, Institute for Domestic and International Policy Studies
Former Minister of Foreign Affairs
Japan

RUDOLPH PENNER
Senior Fellow, The Urban Institute
Former Director, Congressional Budget Office
United States

JESUS SILVA-HERZOG
Former Minister of Finance
Mexico

MARIO HENRIQUE SIMONSEN
Director, Graduate School of Economics, Getúlio Vargas Foundation
Former Minister of Finance and Minister of Planning
Brazil

LUIGI SPAVENTA
Professor of Economics, University of Rome
Former Parliamentary Deputy
Italy

S. C. TSIANG
President, Chung-Hua Institution for Economic Research
Taiwan

MANFRED WEGNER
Director, IFO-Institute for Economic Research
Former Deputy Director General, Commission of the European Community
Federal Republic of Germany

JOHN WILLIAMSON
Senior Fellow, Institute for International Economics
United Kingdom

MASARU YOSHITOMI
Director General, Economic Research Institute, Economic Planning Agency
Former Director, General Economics Branch, Organization for Economic
    Cooperation and Development
Japan

SPECIAL REPORT 6

Resolving the Global Economic Crisis: After Wall Street
Thirty-three Economists from Thirteen Countries

The world economy faces a series of major problems, highlighted by the plunge of the American bond market in early 1987 and the crash of Wall Street and other stock markets later in the year. This detailed statement represents a consensus of top economists from around the world on how to address these issues. It regards the administration-congressional budget deal of late 1987 as "grossly inadequate" and calls for elimination of America's structural budget deficit over the next four years. It also advocates a reduction of $70–100 billion in Japan's trade surplus and suggests that Germany adopt sizable new tax incentives to utilize currently unemployed labor and run current account deficits for awhile. The authors reject the idea that a significant further fall in the dollar would be desirable. Improvements are also suggested for policies in the Asian NICs, the international monetary system, trade policy, and Third World debt.

5 3 5 5

Institute for International Economics
11 Dupont Circle, NW, Washington, DC 20036   ISBN 0–88132–070–6